C000212598

MEEK
BUT MIGHTY

A STUDY OF MOSES

BIBLE STUDIES TO IMPACT THE LIVES
OF ORDINARY PEOPLE

Written by Dorothy Russell

The Word Worldwide

CHRISTIAN FOCUS

For details of our titles visit us on our website
www.christianfocus.com

ISBN 1-85792-951-9

Copyright © WEC International

Published in 2004 by
Christian Focus Publications, Geanies House,
Fearn, Ross-shire, IV20 ITW, Scotland
and
WEC International, Bulstrode, Oxford Road,
Gerrards Cross, Bucks, SL9 8SZ

Cover design by Alister MacInnes

Printed and bound by J W Arrowsmith, Bristol

CONTENTS

QUESTIONS AND NOTES

ANSWER GUIDE

PREFACE
GEARED FOR GROWTH

**'Where there's LIFE there's GROWTH:
Where there's GROWTH there's LIFE.'**

WHY GROW a study group?

Because as we study the Bible and share together we can

- learn to combat loneliness, depression, staleness, frustration, and other problems
- get to understand and love each other
- become responsive to the Holy Spirit's dealing and obedient to God's Word

and that's GROWTH.

How do you GROW a study group?

- Just start by asking a friend to join you and then aim at expanding your group.
- Study the set portions daily (they are brief and easy: no catches).
- Meet once a week to discuss what you find.
- Befriend others, both Christians and non Christians, and work away together

see how it GROWS!

WHEN you GROW ...

This will happen at school, at home, at work, at play, in your youth group, your student fellowship, women's meetings, mid-week meetings, churches and communities,

you'll be REACHING THROUGH TEACHING

INTRODUCTORY STUDY

This time, instead of reading a few verses a day and digging for answers to questions, we are going to read a narrative. One doesn't usually read a story by taking one or two paragraphs at a time! So be ready to READ (it's easier in a modern translation). Read 'The Story of Moses', about one chapter each day, and enjoy finding out more about this Servant of God. It will help you to be a better servant of our Lord Jesus Christ.

What's so special about Moses? What was he like? Let's find out.

Each person could look up one of these verses and read it out:

Exodus 3:11	Deuteronomy 34:5
Exodus 4:10	Psalm 105:26
Numbers 12:3	Deuteronomy 33:1
Numbers 12:7	Deuteronomy 34:10
Hebrews 3:2, 5	Hebrews 11:24-28

Discuss your findings. What kind of a man was Moses? Obviously this is the kind of person God can use.

God made Moses into a strong leader:
  – organizer and pioneer
    – prophet
      – lawgiver
        – literary and spiritual genius

'By the power of God Moses compelled Pharaoh to release a displaced captive audience of two million persons. Then Moses led this timid and easily discouraged horde of ex-slaves through the parted waters of the Red Sea and the rigours of the wilderness. At the end of 40 years, the ex-slaves had been transformed into a disciplined army of warriors, able to smash the opposition of seven powerful and well-armed nations, and to lay claim to the entire land of Canaan which God had promised to Abraham so many centuries before. What leader in all of recorded history can match such an achievement as this?' (*Decision* Magazine, July 1974.)

As you study the life of this great man of God, the use of a commentary will really enrich your study, fill in the background details and make Moses come to life. You will get much more out of the study if you read one alongside your Bible.

STUDY 1

GOD'S PREPARATION

QUESTIONS

DAY 1 *Exodus 2:1-4; Numbers 26:59.*
Meet the family into which Moses was born.
a) What were the names of his father? mother? brother? sister?

b) What nationality were they?

DAY 2 *Exodus 1-2:9; Hebrews 11:23.*
a) What do you think were Moses' mother's feelings when she left him in the basket?

b) What things would she have taught her little boy as she looked after him in the early years?

DAY 3 *Exodus 2:5-10.*
a) How did God work in an unexpected way to save the baby's life and answer his mother's prayers?

b) Can you share with your group some way in which God has answered your prayers?

QUESTIONS (contd.)

DAY 4 *Acts 7:17-23.*
a) Read verse 22 again. What does this verse tell us Moses did while he lived at the Egyptian palace?

b) For how many years was he there?

DAY 5 *Exodus 2:11-15; Acts 7:23-29; Hebrews 11:24-27.*
a) How did Moses feel about his own people, the Hebrews?

b) Read Acts 7:25 again. What was he trying to do?

DAY 6 *Exodus 2:16-22; 18:1-27.*
a) Who did the girls at the well think Moses was? (2:19)

b) What can we discover about Jethro, Moses' father-in-law?

DAY 7 *Exodus 3:1; 17:5; Acts 7:30.*
a) Why would the work of keeping sheep in that area be useful to Moses later on?

b) How long did God spend preparing Moses for this great task?

NOTES

Have you noticed how God used very different kinds of people to have an influence on Moses' life?

... There was his mother
One who loved God, trusted Him for her children, prayed for them and taught them to follow in His ways. A great educator once said, 'Give me a child till he is seven years of age, and I care not who has him afterwards'.

Can you thank God for a mother like this? If so, you have one of the greatest advantages in life? Are you a mother? If so, learn a lesson from Jochebed.

... There was Pharaoh's daughter
Only a link in the chain and not even a worshipper of God, but He used her to save Moses' life and bring him to the place where God wanted him.

When things don't turn out the way we expect, do we remember that God has a plan and we can trust Him?

... There were his instructors
The people he rubbed shoulders with in Egypt. They taught him many things and God planned that it should be so. How else would Moses have been able to stand before Pharaoh with God's message, write the first 5 books of our Bible, compose songs, or organize a rabble of slaves into an army?

We can expect God to teach us things through the people we meet day by day. We can expect Him to use any training or talents we have, in His service.

...There was Jethro
He was a dear old man, with more experience of God than Moses had at that time. Who can tell just how much Moses learned from him over those 40 years! Judging by the later episode, Moses had learned to take his wise advice, too.

Praise God for Christians who are more mature in the faith and wiser than we are! Let's take every opportunity to 'sit at their feet', or ask their advice on our problems – and follow it!

STUDY 2

MOSES' DEPENDENCE ON GOD

QUESTIONS

DAY 1 *Acts 7:30-34; Exodus 3:10.*
a) What did God tell Moses he had planned to do?

b) What was Moses' part in this to be?

DAY 2 *Exodus 3:11–4:17.*
a) How did Moses react to God's plan for him?

b) Why?

DAY 3 *Exodus 4:18–5:21.*
a) How did the people react when Moses and Aaron first told the people of Israel about God's plan?

b) But later, they were angry with Moses and Aaron. Why was there a change in their attitude?

QUESTIONS (contd.)

DAY 4   *Exodus 5:22–6:13.*
a) How do you think Moses was feeling when he brought his problem to the Lord?

b) What do you think God was teaching Moses in these verses?

DAY 5   *Exodus 7:1-13; John 12:47-50.*
Compare these two passages:
a) Who did as God commanded?

b) Who rejected the word of God?

c) Who spoke on God's authority?

DAY 6   *Exodus 7:14–8:32.* The first four plagues.
What impression do you get of Moses in this reading?

DAY 7   *Exodus 9:1–10:29.* The next five plagues.
Have you come across anything in these verses that you did not know before?

NOTES

In Study I we followed Moses' life as he was being trained and prepared for a great task. Now, suddenly, it is upon him, and he was to stand before God, before his own people, and before Pharaoh. Whatever he has already learned is nothing compared with the lessons that God is teaching him now. Let's look at him.

BEFORE GOD

God revealed Himself in a new way and 'Moses hid his face, for he was afraid ...'

Do you remember:

Gideon? – 'Ah, Sovereign Lord! I have seen the angel of the Lord ...' (Judg. 6:22).
Isaiah? – 'Woe to me! ... I am ruined! For I am a man of unclean lips, ...' (Isa. 6:5).
Peter? – 'Go away from me, Lord; I am a sinful man!' (Luke 5:8).

This is how we must all begin, if we want God to use us. He is holy, we are sinful. Have you ever bowed before God's perfect holiness, and acknowledged how worthless you are?

Perhaps it wasn't hard for Moses to agree that he was weak and inadequate, but God then had to teach him what Paul later learned, 'For when I am weak, than I am strong' (2 Cor. 12:10). He was to go, not in his own strength (as he had tried to do 40 years earlier) but in the power of the Almighty, the All-Powerful, the Everlasting God of Abraham, Isaac and Jacob!

And Moses went.

BEFORE HIS OWN PEOPLE

Encouragement   Dear old Aaron was with him again. This was better! He did the speaking and showed the things. And the people believed. A new day of deliverance was coming, and it hadn't been hard, after all.

Discouragement   But later, the people were waiting for them with black looks on their faces. What's this? Things are worse that they were before. God has let them down, and doesn't Moses feel foolish?

Exodus 5:20–6:1:

> As bright hopes fade, stair by stair
> Down plunged the prophet to despair
> His people cruelly misused,
> Their claim for liberty refused,
> Hard works from Pharaoh, and – far worse –

The whiplash of his people's curse.
And, in his hour of utmost need,
God had done nothing, paid no heed –
Then like a flash God's Word broke through,
'Now shalt thou see what I will do.'
Does the dark cloud engulfing you
Seem dense as ever Moses knew?
E'en the next step is hid from view?
All props are knocked from under you,
Your plans have failed, your courage too,
There is naught left that you can do?
On the last rung of the steep stair
That leads straight downward to despair,
This is the Word of God to you,
'Now shalt thou see what I will do.'

BEFORE PHARAOH

By now, it is 'none of self and all of thee'. If Moses had lived in Paul's day, he might have said:

'I have been crucified with Christ
　　it is no longer I who live,
　　　　but Christ who lives in me.'

How else could he possibly have gone in to Pharaoh's court, and asked again the favour that had already brought disastrous results?

STUDY 3

'POWER IN THE BLOOD'

QUESTIONS

DAY 1 *Exodus 11.*
a) Surely Moses has reached the peak of his power as God's instrument now. Which verse tells us this?

b) What was the key to his success? (Heb. 11:28)

DAY 2 *Exodus 12:1-36.*
Read this passage through at least twice, and then write down what impresses you most about it.

DAY 3 *1 Corinthians 5:7; Hebrews 9:22; 1 Peter 1:18, 19; Revelation 5:5-9; 7:13, 14.*
The Passover is a visual aid for us. What must we do, if we want to be freed from the bondage of Satan?

DAY 4 *Exodus 12:37-51; 7:6; 12:28.*
a) What is the 'refrain' that runs through these verses?

b) What is the connection between that and 12:51?

DAY 5   *Exodus 13.*
a) God had another message for Moses. What was it?

b) How did the Lord guide His people in the wilderness?

DAY 6   *Exodus 14.*
a) What did God say to Moses? (v. 2)

b) What did the people say to Moses? (v. 11)

c) What did Moses say to the people? (vv. 13, 14)

d) What did the people believe in? (v. 31)

DAY 7   *Exodus 15:1-21; Revelation 15:3, 4.*
a) Who is Moses' song about?

b) What does it tell us about God?

c) Write down something you can praise God for.

NOTES

Have you got a problem right now?

I'll guarantee it's not quite such a big problem as Moses had! But it may seem just as impossible to solve. So let's see if we can learn from Moses – he saw God doing wonderful things, and so can you.

FAITH

We have seen in our last study how very human Moses was. His faith wavered when he accused God of being slow to act, or not having delivered His people as he had promised (5:23). But God told him to hang on in faith, to trust Him even though he couldn't see the outcome.

God tells us to draw near to Him with a true heart in full assurance of faith and to hold fast the confession of our hope without wavering, for He who promised is faithful (Heb. 10:22, 23).

OBEDIENCE

What a crazy thing to do! Smear blood over your door posts and expect that to keep your oldest son alive. But God had said it, Moses believed it, and that settled it! The people obeyed to the smallest detail what God had told them to do.

We have the Bible, God's Word. It is full of God's commands for us. Are you obeying them? Think of all there is in 2 Corinthians and the other Epistles about the way God wants us to live. In a particular situation, when you ask God for guidance, do you do exactly what he tells you? 'Not as I will, but as you will.'

DELIVERANCE

Oh yes, God will act, when the time is right. We can be absolutely sure of this. We may have to wait, as Moses did, but when the deliverance comes, what a wonderful thing it is! And we realise that it is nothing we could have organized ourselves; all that is required of us is that we 'fear not, stand firm, and see the salvation of the Lord, which He will work for us today'.

PRAISE

'For everything giving thanks in the name of our Lord Jesus Christ to God the Father' (Eph. 5:20).

'He fell on his face at Jesus' feet, giving him thanks' (Luke 17:16).

Don't forget this part, will you? You may not be able to compose a glorious song as Moses did, but the humblest, sincere expression of thanks and praise to God, sounds just as sweet to His ears. When did you last tell Him genuinely how much you loved Him? Our Heavenly Bridegroom longs to hear this from us every bit as much as a husband loves to hear it from his wife.

STUDY 4

GOD TEACHES HIS PEOPLE

QUESTIONS

DAY 1 *Exodus 15:22-27.*
a) 'Moses led Israel' – how did Moses know which way to go?

b) What did they find at Marah? And what at Elim?

DAY 2 *Exodus 16.*
a) When God gave the people manna, how was He testing them?

b) This is the first mention of God's instruction to His people about a 'rest-day', or Sabbath. What is said about it in verse 29?

DAY 3 *Exodus 17:1-7.*
a) What had Moses learned to do when faced with insuperable problems?

b) What reassurance did God give to Moses at this time, which he often used to strengthen His servants? (e.g. Josh. 1:9; Isa. 41:10)

DAY 4 *I Corinthians 10:1-11; John 4:13-14; 7:37-39; Deuteronomy 32:4, 15, 18, 31; Psalm 18:2, 31.*
In what ways is God (Father, Son and Holy Spirit) like the rock?

QUESTIONS (contd.)

DAY 5   *Exodus 17:8-16.*
a) What did the young man Joshua have to do?

b) What was Moses doing?

c) What is this a picture of?

DAY 6   *Exodus 18.*
a) In verses 8-11, what were Moses and Jethro discussing?

b) What change was made in the administration of the community from this point on?

DAY 7   *Exodus 19.*
a) God called Moses up the mountain. What were the two sides of the covenant He proposed? (vv. 5, 6; Rev. 5:9-10)

b) What was God teaching the people by the demonstration recorded in verses 10-24?

NOTES

You can't go this way, though it seems the obvious way to you. Trust me, I know best.

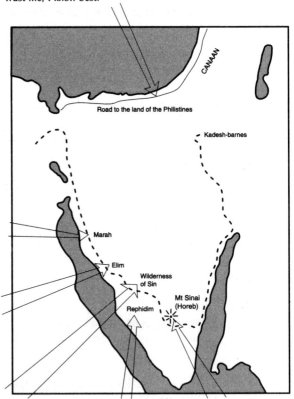

Disappointments may come, but I have the answers. Turn to Me, I can show you what to do.

Be thankful for times of sheer pleasure and refreshing. But remember you are strangers and pilgrims on this earth. Be ready to move on.

Don't be anxious, saying, 'What shall we eat?' Seek first My kingdom and My righteousness, and all these things shall be yours as well.

Daily dependence on me is essential. Don't think you can get very far in your own strength.

I, the Lord, am holy. Do you not know that you are God's temple, and that God's Spirit dwells in you? God's temple is holy, and that temple you are.

STUDY 5

GOD SPEAKS

QUESTIONS

DAY 1 *Exodus 19:24, 25; 20:1-21.*
a) Where was Moses when God spoke the words of the Ten Commandments?

b) Do you remember how Jesus summed up these commandments? (Matt. 22:37-40)

DAY 2 *Deuteronomy 4:10-14; Hebrews 12:18-24.*
a) What did the people see and hear that made them afraid?

b) When we come into God's presence, why need we not be afraid?

DAY 3 *Exodus 21:1-6, 22-27; 22; Matthew 5:38, 39.*
a) Write down briefly one other law that God gave to Moses.

b) Why did Jesus' teaching sometimes differ from Old Testament law?

QUESTIONS (contd.)

DAY 4   *Exodus 24.*
a) When Moses told the people about God's laws, what did they say (twice)?

b) What did God tell Moses to wait for on the mountain?

DAY 5   *Exodus 31:12-18; 32:15, 16.*
a) Which one of the commandments did God repeat before He gave Moses the tablets of stone?

b) Who wrote the commandments on the stones?

DAY 6   *Matthew 5:17-24; Galatians 2:15, 16; 3:24.*
a) Is it possible for a person to keep the Ten Commandments perfectly all his life?

b) Why did God give His people the Law?

DAY 7   *Deuteronomy 5.*
At the end of this chapter, what did Moses advise the people to do?

NOTES

Religion
  Filthy language
    Sunday observance
      Care for the aged
        War
          Sex
            Theft
              Dishonesty
                Materialism

*'The Ten Commandments?
Rather out of date,
don't you think?'*

Pick up today's newspaper. Do you find these topics mentioned?

Why is it that the Ten Commandments are always up to date?

Perhaps it is because, through them, God is speaking to each person as an individual. He does not say, 'People should not ...' he says, 'You (singular) shall not ...'

First he speaks about:

1) my heart
2) my mind
3) my tongue
4) my time
5) my responsibility

1. NO RIVALS FOR GOD

Have you heard of the 'self-made man' who worshipped his makes? I must ask myself, 'Am I putting anything in God's rightful place – money? home? TV? pleasure? sport? church?' If I have to admit that I am, it means that Self is the centre of my life, not God.

*Love God with **all your heart**, and you won't put anything before Him.*

2. NO WRONG IDEAS OF GOD

What is your impression of God? Is He like:

a *Policeman* – enforcing the law and meeting out punishment?
a *Sportsman* – a friendly, indulgent figure who just wants everyone to be happy?
a *Fireman* – to be called upon in a crisis, but not generally needed?
a *Spaceman* – remote, uninterested and out of touch?

Where have you got your impression from?
Could it be that 'your God is too small'?
Are you creating God in your own image?

*Love God **with all your mind** (study His Word intelligently), and you will get a clearer picture of what He is like.*

3. NO SWEARING
There is no place for swearing in a Christian's life.

But some of us never get stirred about God. We tolerate His name being muddied and His teaching mocked, and keep quiet. We may not use His Name in vain, but perhaps we are too afraid to talk about Him at all to others.

*Love God with **all your soul**, and He will control your tongue.*

4. KEEP SUNDAY FOR GOD
Notice that this one is positive, it's a 'do', not a 'don't'. The Jews observed the seventh day as the 'Sabbath' (i.e. 'REST') but the Christians moved it to the first day of the week (Resurrection Day) and called it 'The Lord's Day', and that's the secret. It's a day that we, as Christians, must recognise as belonging to the Lord.

*Love God with **all your strength** and He will show you how to use His Day.*

5. HONOUR YOUR PARENTS
Yes, of course this applies to our children and teenagers, but it applies to us too, while our parents are alive. We have a loving duty to them and part of this duty is to pray regularly for them.

*Love your parents **as yourself** and you will see your responsibility to them.*

* * *

Then God speaks about the things that my neighbour values most:

6) life
7) partner
8) property
9) reputation

6. NO MURDER
Jesus said, 'Under the laws of Moses the rule was, "If you murder, you must die." But I have added to that rule, and will tell you that if you are only angry, even in your own home, you are in danger of judgment!' (Matt. 5:21, 22, LB).

'Anyone who hates his brother is a murderer, and you know that no murderer has eternal life abiding in him' (I John 3:15, RSV).

*Love your neighbour **as yourself** – hatred disappears.*

7. NO ADULTERY

Jesus had something to say about this one, too. He showed us that temptation begins with thoughts. Thoughts of desire, of fun, of a chance of 'happiness', of self-pity. Situations differ, but God's plan for family life still stands.

*Love your neighbour **as yourself**, and you will nip temptation in the bud.*

8. NO STEALING

Of course not!

But what about the time you were undercharged at the supermarket?
Or when the girl gave you change of £10.00 instead of £5.00.
Or when you found that umbrella left in a bus?
And what about making money at someone else's expense? gambling? raffles?
*Love your neighbour **as yourself**, and you won't want to cheat them of anything.*

9. NO LIES

What goes under this heading?

- gossip
- exaggeration
- rumour
- 'white lies'
- deliberate misleading

Perhaps you can add some more.
*Love your neighbour **as yourself**, and you'll have a clear conscience.*

* * *

Finally, God speaks about my inmost thoughts and desires.

10. NO JEALOUSY

Think of it. This is out alongside murder, adultery and the rest! Was God joking? Surely it's not as serious as the others. But when you think carefully, you'll find that jealousy, or covetousness, is often the cause of theft, war, hatred and the like.

It is the spirit of discontent of materialism, of selfishness.

And we must constantly be getting rid of these things in our lives and 'be content with what we have, for he has said, "I will never fail you nor forsake you"' (Heb. 13:5).

*Love your neighbour **as yourself** then it won't matter if they have things that you don't have.*

Lord, give me your kind love.
I can't love you or my neighbour properly in my own strength.
I've tried, and I always fail.
So take over, Lord, You do the loving,
And I'll be the channel.

STUDY 6

MOSES THE INTERCESSOR

QUESTIONS

DAY 1 *Exodus 32:1-10; 20:2-5.*
a) What sin had the people committed while Moses was away?

b) Compare verses 1, 4 and 11 of chapter 32. Who brought the people of Israel out of Egypt?

DAY 2 *Exodus 32:7-14; I Corinthians 10:6-14.*
a) What happened as a result of Israel's sin?

b) Why has God preserved this account down the ages, so that we can read it?

DAY 3 *Exodus 32:7-14; Deuteronomy 9:6-21.*
a) What did the Lord suggest to Moses?

b) What was Moses' reaction?

c) Who did he pray for especially? (Deut. 9:20)

QUESTIONS (contd.)

DAY 4 *Exodus 32:30-35; Deuteronomy 9:24-29; Hebrews 7:25-27.*
a) What did Moses suggest to the Lord, while pleading for the people?

b) What do we read about Jesus, who is our great Deliverer?

DAY 5 *Exodus 33:1-17.*
a) Why did God say He would not go with the people?

b) How did they show they were sorry?

c) What did God agree to do, for Moses' sake? (v. 14)

DAY 6 *Exodus 33:18-34; Deuteronomy 10:1-5.*
a) What did Moses learn about the character of God?

b) Why did God command the Israelites not to make a covenant (peace treaty) with any of the other nations?

DAY 7 *Exodus 34:29-35; Matthew 17:2; Acts 6:15; 2 Corinthians 3:18.*
What do we read about:
   a) Moses?

   b) Christ?

   c) Stephen?

   d) Christians?

NOTES

Has this study brought home to you the seriousness of sin? Are you perhaps horrified at the sin of the Israelites in worshipping the golden calf, but forgetting that God says,

'Yes, **all** have sinned; all fall short of God's glorious ideal'? (Rom. 3:23, LB)

Sin creates a barrier which cuts us off from God for all eternity. We can't come into God's presence unless our sins have been forgiven. Let us therefore realise afresh the meaning of that wonderful verse which says,

'God loved the world so much that he gave his only Son so that anyone who believes in him shall not perish, but have eternal life.'

What Moses could not do for his people, Jesus did for all who trust Him. What Moses did do, was to intercede on behalf of his people. Jesus does this for us today.
Let's look at Moses as he intercedes.

1. Moses knew that, because of God's holy and righteous character, He must punish sin. Perhaps he didn't know what was later revealed to the prophet Hosea, that God's heart 'recoiled within him' at the thought (Hos. 11:8, ESV).

2. Moses heard God's suggestion – 'I will destroy the people, but of you I will make a great nation.' It was God testing His servant very much in the same way he tested Abraham (Gen. 22:1, 2). Why?
    When the devil tempts us, it is to try to make us do wrong; when God tests us it is to try to bring out the best in us. Moses responded magnificently to the test.

3. What was Moses' motive in pleading for his people? This is all-important. Was it just so that the people would live to enjoy life a bit longer? Moses first reminds God of how He has lovingly cared for these people in the past, then he imagines how God's enemies would mock Him if he destroyed them, thirdly he tells God that because He is God, He must keep His promises. In short, his motive for pleading was God's ultimate glory.
    Why do you pray for others?

4. As Intercessor, Moses perfectly identified himself with the people. We know of another who 'was numbered with the transgressors' (Isa. 53:12). Most people know very little about intercessory prayer. In *Rees Howells – Intercessor* by Norman Grubb we read of Mr

Howells (ch. 12, 'What is an Intercessor?') –

'He pleads effectively because he gives his life for those he pleads for; he is their genuine representative; he has submerged self-interest in their needs and sufferings, and as far as possible has literally taken their place.'

5. Dear Moses! How God must have loved him for that willingness to sacrifice himself. But there was something Moses did not know. Forgiveness by God was and is rendered possible only by the fact that Christ died to take the punishment for sin. That included this sin of the Israelites, for God is timeless, and Christ's atonement was just as effective in retrospect as it is for us today (Rom. 3:25).

6. 'My presence will go with you, and I will give you rest.' If God is dwelling within us and goes with us, we must be cleansed from sin, as the Israelites were. It is only when we are cleansed from sin that we can have His rest or peace of mind. Don't you find this true, from your experience?

7. Did Moses really change God's mind? Doesn't the Bible say that God repented? *The New Bible Commentary* (The Inter-Varsity Press 1953, p. 129) is helpful here: 'God does not repent as men do, as though He had erred or was too weak-minded to carry out His purposes. When God "repents" He changes, not His eternal purposes, but the course of events which He had previously stated, because the prayers or altered demeanour of His people alter the conditions under which He had originally made that statement.'

STUDY 7

THE TABERNACLE

QUESTIONS

DAY 1 *Exodus 24.*

a) What helped you most, or was new to you, in last week's study?

b) What special preparation did Moses have before receiving the instructions for the Tabernacle?

DAY 2 *Exodus 25:1-9; 3:22; 12:35, 36.*

a) How did the Israelites get the materials to make the Tabernacle?

b) What was God's purpose in having it built?

DAY 3 *Exodus 35:1-9, 20-35; 31:1-6.*

a) Which verses tell us that the people gave of their own free will?

b) How were Bezalel and Oholiab specially fitted for the work God gave them?

DAY 4 *Exodus 25:10-30; 37:1-16.*

a) What did the Ark look like?

b) What was to be kept on the golden table?

QUESTIONS (contd.)

DAY 5   *Exodus 25:31-40; 37:17-24; Hebrews 8:5.*
a) Can you describe (or draw) the lampstand?

b) What command did God give to Moses about the building of the Tabernacle?

DAY 6   *Exodus 26:1-17, 30-36; 36:1-20, 35.*
a) What was the tent part of the Tabernacle to be made from?

b) What was the roof to be made from?

c) What was the framework to be made from?

d) What was the veil to be made from?

DAY 7   *Exodus 27:1-5; 29:38-46.*
a) What was the bronze altar to be used for?

b) Exodus 30:1-9. What was the smaller, golden altar to be used for?

c) Exodus 30:17-20; 38:8. What was the bronze basin (or laver) for?

d) What was it made from?

NOTES

Let us approach with reverence that structure, planned by God as a huge visual aid to teach His people eternal truths. What a picture it is of Christ, His life, His death, and His love for us!

The Outer Coverings were unattractive, and we read of Christ, 'He had no form or comeliness. He was despised and rejected by men' (Isa. 53:2, 3).

The Inner Curtains, however, were of great beauty and significance.

Blue – the colour of the heavens, speaks of His Divinity.

Scarlet – the colour of the Palestinian earth, shows His Humanity.

Purple – the mixing of blue and scarlet together, shows the perfect blending of human and divine, and reminds us that He is the only mediator between God and man.

Purple is also the royal colour for the King of Kings.

Fine twined linen – reminds us of His pure, spotless, perfect life!

We enter through the gate, and the first thing we see in the outer court is the **Bronze Altar**. This altar of sacrifice was to teach the people that 'without the shedding of blood there is no forgiveness of sins' (Heb. 9.22). Salvation is costly, and we should not forget that we have been redeemed 'with the precious blood of Christ' (I Pet. 1:19). Hebrews 10:1-18 gives a fuller comment. Christ offered Himself once and for all, as a sacrifice for sin, and we must accept this for ourselves before we can go any further.

Next we come to the **Bronze Basin**, for ceremonial washing. The cleansing with water speaks to the believer of a life of holiness and sanctification through His Word.

Jesus said, 'You are clean because of the word I have spoken to you' (John 15:3). He prayed, 'Sanctify them by the truth; your word is truth' (John 17:7). Ephesians 5:26 reads, 'Christ loved the church and gave himself up for her to make her holy, cleansing her by the washing with water through the word.'

And the question, 'How can a young man keep his way pure?' is answered, 'By living according to your word' (Ps. 119:9).

We enter the Holy Place, and on our left stands the **Lampstand**. Made of solid gold, hammered and beaten into a thing of great beauty, this again turns our eyes upon Jesus, the Light of the world, of whom it was written, 'Yet it was the will of the Lord to bruise Him.' The Lampstand shows the unity of believers, one in Him. He is the vine, we are the branches, and so, too, are called to be lights that shine before men. Notice that the branches and the shaft are all of one piece, and all of pure, beaten gold. Job said, 'he knows the way that I take; when He has tested me, I shall come forth as gold' (Job 23:10).

On our right is the **Golden Table**. This table was made of common acacia wood, which grew just where the people were. This symbolized Christ's humanity, and showed that He lived with men and for men. But it was overlaid with pure gold, showing His divinity. The bread was made of the finest wheat, ground, sieved and tested, and was to be renewed every Sabbath. What a picture of our fellowship with Jesus, the Bread of Life, and especially of Communion with Him at the Lord's Table!

At the end of the Holy Place, we can see the veil, or curtain which separates us from the Holy of Holies. But in front of the veil we see the **Altar of Incense**. Its position is important, as it was the nearest point to God's presence that the priest could go. Incense stands for prayer (e.g., 'golden bowls full of incense which are the prayers of the saints' spoken of in Rev. 5:8). This altar was also made of wood and gold, and we see the man Christ Jesus who 'ever lives to make intercession for us.'

Aaron was to burn the incense morning and evening, to keep a perpetual fragrance in the Holy Place, and God waits for the sweet aroma of our prayers to ascend to Him daily, so that we can spread 'everywhere the fragrance of the knowledge of him' (2 Cor. 2:14).

The Veil

Hebrews 10:20 tells us that the veil was a type of Christ's body. 'The Word was made flesh and dwelt (or "tabernacled") among us' (John 1:14).

The heavenly blue reminds us that the angel said to Mary, 'The child to be born will be called Holy, Son of God'. Yet the red of the earth shows that He was born of woman, the Son of Man. The blending of the purple foreshadows the prophecy in Isaiah, 'His name shall be called Emmanuel, God with us.'

The purpose of the Veil in the Tabernacle was to keep man at a distance from God, but we know that when Christ's body was broken on the Cross, the Veil of the Temple was rent in two (Matt. 27:51) and a new and living way was opened for us into God's holy presence (Heb. 10:20).

With reverence and holy awe we step beyond the veil into the Holiest of all, and gaze upon the **Ark of the Covenant**, a thing the Old Testament saints were never permitted to do.

Inside the Ark are the tablets of stone with the law written on them, a reminder of our sin. Above the Ark is the glory of a pure and holy God, the God who cannot look upon sin. And in between ... is the Mercy Seat, God's gracious mercy to me in providing a covering for my sin. 'Blessed is the man whose iniquity is forgiven, whose sin is covered!' How wonderful that God's love and God's justice can be so fully satisfied in the perfect atonement of our Saviour. 'Let us then with confidence draw near to the throne of grace, that we may receive mercy, and find grace to help in time of need' (Heb. 4:16).

STUDY 8

BEWARE OF UNBELIEF

QUESTIONS

DAY 1   *Exodus 40:16-38; 2 Chronicles 7:1-3.*
a) What is the 'refrain' that is repeated 8 times in this chapter?

b) What filled the Tabernacle when the work was completed?

DAY 2   *Numbers 9:15-23; 10:33-36; John 8:12.*
a) How did the Israelites know when to move on and where to go?

b) How does the Christian know what is right, and what to do with his life?

DAY 3   *Deuteronomy 1:6-8, 19-25; Numbers 13:17-26.*
a) What did God, through Moses, command the people to do when they arrived at Kadesh Barnea?

b) Instead of doing this, what did they do?

DAY 4   *Numbers 13:27-33; Hebrews 3:7-19.*
a) What did ten of the spies report?

b) What did Caleb and Joshua say?

c) What did the people decide?

DAY 5 *Deuteronomy 1:26-40; Hebrews 3:7-19.*
a) Who did God say could not enter the land?

b) Why? (v. 32)

c) Who did He say would enter the land?

DAY 6 *Numbers 14:10-39.*
a) What part that we have already studied, does Moses' behaviour remind you of?

b) Did God pardon the people?

c) Did they have to suffer the consequence of their sin?

DAY 7 *Hebrews 4:1-11; 2 Corinthians 6:2.*
a) What can we learn from the story we have read this week?

b) What do you think is the 'rest' mentioned here? (see Matt. 11:28)

NOTES

'Take care, brethren, ...' (Heb. 3:12) RSV.
'You should therefore be most careful, my brothers ...' Phillips.
'See to it, brothers ...' NEB.
'My fellow-believers, be careful ...' GNB.
'Beware then of your own hearts ...' LB.

It does not matter which translation you use, the warning is clear. We are to beware of unbelief. It is a solemn thought. Yet all through the Bible we find that it is the prime sin, and it brings dreadful consequences.

Genesis 3:3, 4	'God said, "You shall not eat of the fruit which is in the midst of the garden, neither shall you touch it, lest you die.; But the serpent said to the woman, "You will not die."'
2 Kings 17:13, 14	Again and again the Lord sent prophets to warn both Israel and Judah to turn them from their evil ways but Israel wouldn't listen ... and refused to believe in the Lord their God.
Matthew 13:58	'And he (Jesus) did not do many miracles there because of their lack of faith.'
Mark 16:14	He rebuked them for their unbelief – their stubborn refusal to believe those who had seen Him alive from the dead.
John 16:8, 9	'When he (the Holy Spirit) comes, he will convict the world of guilt in regard to sin and unrighteousness ... because men do not believe in me ...'

UNBELIEF and **DISOBEDIENCE** are two sides of the same coin. If we don't believe God's word, we won't obey it. Do we really believe God when He says:

'Come unto Me and I will give you rest'? Do we come?
'It is more blessed to give than receive'? Do we give?
'All things work together for good to them that love God'? Do we trust Him?

And so we could go on. As we read our Bibles day by day, let us keep a check on ourselves: 'Take care, brethren, lest there be in any of you an evil, unbelieving heart.'

Rather let us be like Abraham: 'Abraham never doubted. He believed God, for his faith and trust grew ever stronger, and he praised God for this blessing (a son in his old age) even before it happened. He was completely sure that God was well able to do anything he promised' (Rom. 4:20, 21).

STUDY 9

GRUMBLINGS

QUESTIONS

As you do the questions, make a list of the things the people grumbled about during their wanderings.

DAY 1 *Numbers 11.*
a) Grumbling 1 and 2 are in this section. What are they?

b) What were the two punishments God sent?

DAY 2 *Numbers 12.*
a) Grumbling number 3 – who grumbled? What about?

b) What did Moses do?

DAY 3 *Numbers 14:1-4, 40-45.*
a) Grumbling 4 and 5. Add them to your list (vv. 2, 3, 40).

b) What was wrong with the people's reasoning in verse 40?

QUESTIONS (contd.)

DAY 4 *Numbers 16.*
a) Two more grumblings in this chapter (vv. 3, 10(b), 41).

b) What strikes you most about this story?

DAY 5 *Numbers 20:1-13.*
a) Have you noticed what Moses does every time the people grumble?

b) What did Moses do that was not exactly as God had commanded? (Don't forget to add Grumbling 8.)

DAY 6 *I Corinthians 10:1-12; Deuteronomy 32:4; John 7:38, 39.*
a) Of whom was the rock a symbol?

b) What does the New Testament warn us against?

DAY 7 *Deuteronomy 29:5; Numbers 21:4-9; John 3:14, 15.*
a) What were the people grumbling about this time? (No. 9)?

b) How was the serpent on the pole a picture of Christ?

NOTES

The people complained about:

The hardships God allowed them to endure – 'If only circumstances were different!'
The situations in which they found themselves – 'Remember the good old days?'
The fact that someone else was better off than they were – 'Why choose Moses?'
God's judgment upon them – 'It's not fair ... Why me?'
God's provision for them – 'For what we are about to receive – ugh!'

We have seen what God's feelings were about the sin of grumbling. We need to recognize this as sin, so if this passage convicts you, tell the Lord about it. He is faithful and just, and He will forgive you.

* * *

Moses was a man greatly beloved by God, spoken of by Him as 'my servant', and one with whom He spoke face to face. Yet Moses was not perfect. The Bible never glosses over the sins of its great men, and perhaps this is for our encouragement.

Moses was told to speak to the rock. He disobeyed. We saw last week that disobedience and unbelief go hand in hand, and we are warned to be on our guard.
Did Moses think he knew better than God?
Did he not have enough faith to believe that what God had told him to do would work?
Did he think he could produce the water himself by physical means? Did temper get the better of him?

Moses was only required to obey, he could see no further.
But we know that the rock was a picture of Christ. When Moses was told to smite the rock, the first time, is a picture of Christ crucified, necessary for our salvation. But this time he was to speak to the rock – a picture of Christ alive, risen from the dead, and giving the water of life freely to all who come to him.

* * *

God gave His people another object lesson when they were being bitten by the poisonous snakes.
Things were clear cut: Either you turned and looked at the brass serpent – or you died. It may have seemed ridiculous, and some may not have believed it would work, but they had to choose whether they would have faith in God's remedy or not, and choose quickly before it was too late!
The lesson for us today is clear, isn't it?
Amos' message was 'Seek the Lord and live!' Surely it is only foolishness to turn our backs on the Saviour who was lifted up on the cross to die, so that we might live. There is no other way to have eternal life.

STUDY 10

THE MOUNTAIN-TOP EXPERIENCE

QUESTIONS

DAY 1 *Numbers 27:12-19; Deuteronomy 31:14.*
a) What was one reason why Moses was not allowed to enter the Promised Land?

b) What was Moses' first concern when he knew it was time for him to die?

DAY 2 *Deuteronomy 1:21, 26, 32, 37; 3:23-29.*
a) What other reason is given for Moses not entering the Promised Land?

b) Discuss why God did not agree to Moses' earnest pleading this time.

DAY 3 *Deuteronomy 31:1-8; Joshua 1:5-9.*
a) How old was Moses at this time?

b) What was his message to Joshua (repeated later by God)?

QUESTIONS (contd.)

DAY 4 *Deuteronomy 31:9-13; 11:18, 19; 32:45-47.*
a) Why was it important that the children should learn God's law?

b) Do you think it is important today for parents to teach children about God, or is it enough to send them to Sunday School?

DAY 5 *Deuteronomy 31:24-29; Hebrews 8:8-10.*
a) Where did Moses command that the book of the Law should be placed?

b) Where does God intend that His law should be today?

DAY 6 *Deuteronomy 31:19-22; 32:1-15* (or to the end of the song if possible).
a) Why was Moses told to write this song?

b) What did God realise the people would do in later generations?

DAY 7 *Deuteronomy 32:48-52; 34.*
a) What last pleasure did God give to Moses before he died?

b) Look up chapter 33:27. In what way can this verse comfort those who have been bereaved?

NOTES

Have you noticed how sacred were the times when Moses met God on the mountain tops?

Exodus 3   God commissioned him for his life's work, by calling to him from the burning bush on Mt Horeb.

Exodus 19   Repeatedly, Moses climbed Mt Sinai (Horeb) to talk with God face to face, to receive the Ten Commandments and the instructions for the Tabernacle, and to plead for the people.

Deuteronomy 34   From Mt Nebo, God showed him the Promised Land, and then took him to Heaven, to be with Himself.

Mark 9   The next time Moses appears in Scripture, he is on the Mount of Transfiguration with Jesus and Elijah, discussing the events of the crucifixion, which would make perfect atonement for man's sin.

* * *

From Mt Nebo, Moses could see the land of Canaan, but he was not allowed to enter. Yet he was taken by God to 'a better country, that is, a heavenly one' (Heb. 11:16) where all his longings were satisfied.

How wonderful to see him, in Christ's day, in the very land which he had so much desired to enter! And what is he doing? He is talking with his Lord face to face.

* * *

In a lovely little book by Jessie Penn-Lewis called *Face to Face* she writes about Moses and his intimate fellowship with God:

> 'Face to face fellowship means that anywhere, at any moment we may converse with Him who is invisible, and hear His voice in our hearts speaking to us across the blood-sprinkled Mercy-Seat.'

> 'The Lord talked with Moses face to face, as a man speaks to his friend' (Exod. 33:11).

And what is death, for one who loves his Lord?
It is 'face to face with Christ my Saviour' in a closeness that we can scarcely imagine.

'Absent from the body, present with the Lord' (2 Cor. 5:8).
'Now we see in a mirror dimly, but then face to face' (I Cor. 13:12).
'We shall be like him, for we shall see him as he is' (I John 3:2).
'His servants shall worship him; they shall see his face' (Rev. 22:4, 5).

If to die is to rise in power from the husk of the earth's own wheat,
If to die is to rise in glory from the dust of the incomplete;
If death is the end to all sorrow and crying and anxious care,
If death gives fullness for longing, and answer to every prayer;
If death is to greet all the martyrs and prophets and sages of old,
And to walk again by still waters with the flocks of our own little fold;
If to die is to join in Hosannas to a risen and reigning Lord,
And to feast with Him at His table, on the bread and wine of His board;
If to die is to enter a city and be hailed as a child of its King –
    O grave, where soundeth thy triumph?
    O death, where is thy sting?

ANSWER GUIDE

The following pages contain an Answer Guide. It is recommended that answers to the questions be attempted before turning to this guide. It is only a guide and the answers given should not be treated as exhaustive.

GUIDE TO INTRODUCTORY STUDY

For the first meeting, it is suggested that you give out pencils and paper and challenge your group with this Quiz! (Keep it light hearted and remember it may be quite difficult for some people.) Then go on to the Introductory Study Sheet.

QUIZ

1. Who found Moses, when, as a baby, he was put in a basket among the bulrushes?
2. Later, when he had left Egypt God spoke to him in a strange way. What did he see that attracted his attention?
3. What was the name given to the feast that the people of Israel kept just before they were led out of bondage in Egypt?
4. How did they get across the Red Sea?
5. When Moses talked with God on Mount Sinai, what did God give him?
6. What had the people made, to worship, when Moses stayed away so long?
7. Moses got instructions from God for making a worship centre in the wilderness. What was it called?
8. When the people first reached the borders of the Promised Land, they sent in spies. What did the spies report?
9. Because they did not believe God or trust Him, the people had to wander in the wilderness for many years – how many?
10. Did Moses actually go into the Promised Land?

GUIDE TO STUDY 1

DAY 1   a) Amram, Jochebed, Aaron, Miriam.
b) Hebrews.

DAY 2   a) It was by 'faith' that she hid him and was not afraid. All natural feelings were superseded by her faith.
b) The history of his people, the worship of God, the promise that God would bring His people out of bondage (Gen. 15:13, 14).

DAY 3   a) He used the Egyptian princess with her natural womanly instincts.
b) Personal.

DAY 4   a) He would have had a tutor and been educated in a highly civilized society. 'powerful in speech' implies that he was a statesman, perhaps orator; 'powerful ... in action' points to valour in battle, etc.
b) Until he was 40.

DAY 5   a) Indignant at the way they were being treated.
b) He was trying to begin a deliverance from their bondage.

DAY 6   a) An Egyptian.
b) He was hospitable, polite, and he loved the Lord. He and Moses had a close relationship, he was concerned for Moses, and he gave him good advice.

DAY 7   a) He must have got to know the country, the conditions, waterholes, etc. (Mt Horeb and Mt Sinai are the same.)
b) 80 years.

GUIDE TO STUDY 2

DAY 1   a) Bring His people out of bondage in Egypt to the Promised Land.
b) He was to go to Pharaoh, and ultimately lead the people out.

DAY 2   a) He made excuses: Who am I? (3:11)
What shall I tell them? (3:13)
They won't believe me! (4:1)
I'm not a good speaker. ((4:10)
b) He didn't want to go because he was afraid, felt inadequate or perhaps didn't want to be disturbed out of his comfortable rut.

DAY 3   a) They believed and worshipped. (4:31)
b) Their work had been made heavier; it looked as though God's plan had not worked.

DAY 4   a) Discouraged, miserable, resentful.
b) That he was all-powerful and His plan was going to work.

DAY 5   a) Moses and Aaron, Jesus
b) Pharaoh.
c) Moses and Aaron, Jesus.

DAY 6   Obedient to the word of the Lord. Calm, confident and polite before Pharaoh, but uncompromising.

DAY 7   Personal.

GUIDE TO STUDY 3

DAY 1   a) Verse 3
              b) Faith

DAY 2   Personal

DAY 3   Personally accept the atoning sacrifice of Christ, recognizing that only by His blood can we be made clean to stand before Him. (This could be an opportunity to discuss the way of salvation with your group.)

DAY 4   a) They did as the Lord commanded.
              b) Only because of their obedience could the Lord work His mighty act of deliverance.

DAY 5   a) To tell the people to keep the Passover as a reminder of what God had done for them. (Note especially v. 8.)
              b) By a pillar of cloud by day and a pillar of fire by night.

DAY 6   a) To camp by the sea.
              b) They asked why they had been brought to the desert to die.
              c) To not fear and stand firm and still to see God's deliverance.
              d) The Lord and his servant Moses.

DAY 7   a) God.
              b) That He is all-powerful, majestic, holy, etc.
              c) Personal.

GUIDE TO STUDY 4

DAY 1
a) The pillar of cloud and fire. (13:21)
b) Marah – bitter water. Elim – 12 springs of water, 70 palm trees.

DAY 2
a) To see if they would keep His commands (see v. 28).
b) It was a God-given gift.

DAY 3
a) Bring his problem to the Lord (v. 4).
b) 'I will stand there before you' (v. 6), i.e., 'I will be with you'.

DAY 4
Christ was the Rock who was smitten, to give the water of life.
The 'streams of living water' symbolises the Holy Spirit.
God is sure, strong and unmovable – 'Rock of Ages, cleft for me'.

DAY 5
a) Lead the battle against the Amalekites.
b) Holding up his hands to God on behalf of the people.
c) Prayer.

DAY 6
a) All that the Lord had done.
b) Judges were appointed for ordinary matters; Moses confined himself to the 'hard cases'.

DAY 7
a) The people were to obey God's voice. God would make them a kingdom of priests and a holy nation.
b) That He was holy, majestic, Spirit and Supreme Lord.

GUIDE TO STUDY 5

DAY 1   a) With the people at the foot of the Mount. (Look up Heb. 1:1 about how God speaks.)
b) Love God with all your heart, soul and mind. Love your neighbour as yourself.

DAY 2   a) Saw – the mountain burning with fire, darkness, cloud, gloom. Heard – God's voice.
b) We need not be afraid because we come to the heavenly Jerusalem, and to Jesus who made this possible for us by His death.

DAY 3   a) May be any one given in these verses – (the whole book of Leviticus records more laws, see Lev. 27:34).
b) Because He was fulfilling the Law, showing us the spirit of the Law as well as the letter.

DAY 4   a) That they would do and obey everything God had said.
b) The laws written on tablets of stone.

DAY 5   a) Remember the Sabbath Day, to keep it holy.
b) God.

DAY 6   a) No.
b) To teach and guide them until Christ came.

DAY 7   Obey all the commandments of the Lord.

GUIDE TO STUDY 6

DAY 1
a) Idolatry. Worshipping God in the form of an image, expressly forbidden.
b) God had brought them out under the leadership of Moses.

DAY 2
a) Tablets of stone broken deliberately (to symbolize the breaking of the commandments). Moses melted the calf, ground it to powder, sprinkled it on the water and made the people drink it. Aaron lied and tried to excuse himself. 3,000 men were killed (A similar sin is referred to in Num. 25:1-9 where 24,000 were killed.)
b) So that we can be warned against falling into sin.

DAY 3
a) That he would destroy the people and make a great nation of Moses and his descendants instead (Exod. 32:10; Deut. 9:14).
b) He begged God not to do this; he reminded God of His promise to Abraham, Isaac and Jacob.
c) Aaron.

DAY 4
a) He suggested that he himself might be offered as a sacrifice to atone for the people's sin.
b) He offered Himself as a ransom for our sin. Jesus is continually making intercession for us.

DAY 5
a) Because they were unruly and stubborn and He would be tempted to destroy them.
b) They went into mourning and took off their ornaments.
c) God agreed that His presence would go with them and He would give them rest (or success).

DAY 6
a) That He was holy, inexhaustible in love, abounding in mercy and forgiveness towards those who walk in His ways, but just and righteous and executing judgment upon those who don't.
b) Because the other nations would then lead God's people into further sin and idolatry.

DAY 7
a) Moses: the skin of his face shone because he had been talking with God.
b) Christ: His face shone like the sun on the mountain.
c) Stephen: his face became as radiant as an angel's.
d) Christians: we can become more and more like Christ as we behold His glory.

GUIDE TO STUDY 7

DAY 1
a) Personal.
b) He was given a revelation of God in His glory.

DAY 2
a) They got them from the Egyptians.
b) So that he could dwell in their midst.

DAY 3
a) Verses 5, 21, 22, 29.
b) They were filled with the Spirit of God, and with ability, intelligence, knowledge and craftsmanship, and were also inspired by God to teach others these things.

DAY 4
a) The Ark was a rectangular box, 1.1 x 0.7 x 0.7 metres, made of wood and covered inside and out with gold. The lid (mercy-seat) was a gold plate with a winged cherub at each end.
b) Plates, dishes and bowls of gold, and the 'bread of the Presence'.

DAY 5
a) Made of gold, with 7 branches and 7 lights. (Bring along a picture, if possible.)
b) It was to be made according to the pattern shown to Moses on the mountain (see also Exod. 25:9).

DAY 6
a) Ten curtains of linen, and blue, purple and scarlet material.
b) Curtains of goats' hair with tanned rams' skins and goatskins (or badger skins) on top.
c) Acacia wood.
d) Blue, purple and scarlet material, and fine linen.

DAY 7
a) Sacrifices.
b) Burning incense.
c) Ceremonial washing.
d) The women's mirrors.

GUIDE TO STUDY 8

DAY 1 a) Moses did ... as the Lord commanded him.
b) The glory of the Lord, seen in a cloud by day and a fire by night.

DAY 2 a) When the cloud lifted from the Tabernacle, the people moved on, when it stayed, they camped. In this way the Lord instructed them. (Bring out how this made them depend completely on God.)
b) The Christian must also depend completely on Jesus for guidance, and so be enabled to walk in the light.

'Dear Lord, of Thee three things I pray – to see Thee more clearly, love Thee more dearly, follow Thee more nearly day by day.'

DAY 3 a) Go in and take possession of Canaan, the Promised Land.
b) They sent spies in first to see what the land was like.

DAY 4 a) It is a good land, but the people are too strong for us.
b) It is a good land, and the Lord will bring us in.
c) Not to go in.

DAY 5 a) All the adult people (including Moses) except Caleb and Joshua.
b) Because they did not believe what God had said.
c) Caleb, Joshua, and the children, when grown up.

DAY 6 a) Moses interceding for the people after the sin of the golden calf (Exod. 32, 33).
b) Yes.
c) Yes.

DAY 7 a) That we should make quite sure that we are among those who will enter God's rest (Heb. 4:1,11). That the reason for not entering is unbelief (Heb. 4:2, 3).
b) Those who find salvation and new life in Christ cease from their own works (as God did on the seventh day of creation) and find rest and peace in Him, here and now, as well as looking forward to the joys of heaven (Rev. 14:13).

MOSES • ANSWER GUIDE

GUIDE TO STUDY 9

DAY 1   a) Grumble 1 was about the way God had led them.
Grumble 2 was about the food God sent.
b) Fire and plague.

DAY 2   a) Grumble 3 – Miriam and Aaron complained about Moses being chosen as leader.
b) Moses prayed for them.

DAY 3   a) Grumble 4 was about the land where they were.
Grumble 5 was about God's decision not to let them go into Canaan.
b) They were too late – God's judgment had already been pronounced.

DAY 4   a) Grumble 6 was about Moses being leader and Aaron priest.
Grumble 7 was about Moses' (or rather God's) judgment on Korah
b) Personal. (Perhaps the fierceness of God's judgment on this sin.)

DAY 5   a) He takes his problems to the Lord in prayer.
b) He struck the rock twice instead of speaking to it.
Grumble 8 was about the lack of water.

DAY 6   a) Christ.
b) Desiring evil, worshipping idols, immorality, putting the Lord to the test, grumbling, and thinking we are safe from these things.

DAY 7   a) Grumble 9. About the food God had provided.
b) He was lifted up on the Cross, and through trusting in His death to save us, we have eternal life.

GUIDE TO STUDY 10

DAY 1   a) Disobedience – the striking the rock at Meribah.
b) He wanted God to appoint a leader in his place, so that the people would not be like sheep without a shepherd. (See John 10:11-14.)

DAY 2   a) Unbelief – Moses, with the people, did not believe that they could conquer the land.
b) Moses said, 'Let me go over and see ...' God said no to the first part, but yes to the second.
Sin may be forgiven, but the consequences remain.
Moses symbolizes the Law, which can never lead people into God's rest. Perhaps God wanted to teach Moses, like Paul, that His grace was sufficient (2 Cor. 12:8, 9).

DAY 3   a) 120 years old.
b) Be strong and of good courage, for the Lord will not fail you.

DAY 4   a) So that they would learn to fear and obey the Lord while they lived in the land He had given them. This would bring life and blessing.
b) Very important a child's home in his training ground; Sunday School is only one hour per week.

DAY 5   a) In the ark of the covenant.
b) In our minds and hearts.

DAY 6   a) As we witness (warning or reminder) to the people.
b) Forget Him.

DAY 7   a) Moses saw all the Promised Land from a distance.
b) It reminds us that God is eternal, unchangeable, and a refuge for all who seek Him. However low we sink in the depths of despair, He is always able to lift us up.

OLD TESTAMENT

Triumphs Over Failures: A Study in Judges ISBN 1-85792-888-1
Messenger of Love: A Study in Malachi ISBN 1-85792-885-7
The Beginning of Everything: A Study in Genesis 1-11 ISBN 0-90806-728-3
Hypocrisy in Religion: A Study in Amos ISBN 0-90806-706-2
Unshakeable Confidence: A Study in Habakkuk & Joel ISBN 0-90806-751-8
A Saviour is Promised: A Study in Isaiah 1 - 39 ISBN 0-90806-755-0
The Throne and Temple: A Study in 1 & 2 Chronicles ISBN 1-85792-910-1
Our Magnificent God: A Study in Isaiah 40 - 66 ISBN 1-85792-909-8
The Cost of Obedience: A Study in Jeremiah ISBN 0-90806-761-5
Focus on Faith: A Study of 10 Old Testament Characters ISBN 1-85792-890-3
Faith, Courage and Perserverance: A Study in Ezra ISBN 1-85792-949-7

NEW TESTAMENT

The World's Only Hope: A Study in Luke ISBN 1-85792-886-5
Walking in Love: A Study in John's Epistles ISBN 1-85792-891-1
Faith that Works: A Study in James ISBN 0-90806-701-1
Made Completely New: A Study in Colossians & Philemon ISBN 0-90806-721-6
Jesus-Christ, Who is He? A Study in John's Gospel ISBN 0-90806-716-X
Entering by Faith: A Study in Hebrews ISBN 1-85792-914-4
Heavenly Living: A Study in Ephesians ISBN 1-85792-911-X
The Early Church: A Study in Acts 1-12 ISBN 0-90806-736-4
The Only Way to be Good: A Study in Romans ISBN 1-85792-950-0
Get Ready: A Study in 1 & 2 Thessalonians ISBN 1-85792-948-9

CHARACTERS

Abraham: A Study of Genesis 12-25 ISBN 1-85792-887-3
Serving the Lord: A Study of Joshua ISBN 1-85792-889-X
Achieving the Impossible: A Study of Nehemiah ISBN 0-90806-707-0
God plans for Good: A Study of Joseph ISBN 0-90806-700-3
A Man After God's Own Heart: A Study of David ISBN 0-90806-746-1
Grace & Grit: A Study of Ruth & Esther ISBN 1-85792-908-X
Men of Courage: A Study of Elijah & Elisha ISBN 1-85792-913-6

THEMES

God's Heart, My Heart: World Mission ISBN 1-85792-892-X
Freedom: You Can Find it! ISBN 0-90806-702-X
Freely Forgiven: A Study in Redemption ISBN 0-90806-720-8
The Problems of Life! Is there an Answer? ISBN 1-85792-907-1
Understanding the Way of Salvation ISBN 0-90082-880-3
Saints in Service: 12 Bible Characters ISBN 1-85792-912-8
Finding Christ in the Old Testament: Pre-existence and Prophecy ISBN 0-90806-739-9

THE WORD WORLDWIDE

We first heard of WORD WORLDWIDE over 20 years ago when Marie Dinnen, its founder, shared excitedly about the wonderful way ministry to one needy woman had exploded to touch many lives. It was great to see the Word of God being made central in the lives of thousands of men and women, then to witness the life-changing results of them applying the Word to their circumstances. Over the years the vision for WORD WORLDWIDE has not dimmed in the hearts of those who are involved in this ministry. God is still at work through His Word and in today's self-seeking society, the Word is even more relevant to those who desire true meaning and purpose in life. WORD WORLDWIDE is a ministry of WEC International, an interdenominational missionary society, whose sole purpose is to see Christ known, loved and worshipped by all, particularly those who have yet to hear of His wonderful name. This ministry is a vital part of our work and we warmly recommend the WORD WORLDWIDE 'Geared for Growth' Bible studies to you. We know that as you study His Word you will be enriched in your personal walk with Christ. It is our hope that as you are blessed through these studies, you will find opportunities to help others discover a personal relationship with Jesus. As a mission we would encourage you to work with us to make Christ known to the ends of the earth.

Stewart and Jean Moulds – British Directors, **WEC International.**

A full list of over 50 'Geared for Growth' studies can be obtained from:

John and Ann Edwards
5 Louvaine Terrace, Hetton-le-Hole, Tyne & Wear, DH5 9PP
Tel. 0191 5262803 Email: rhysjohn.edwards@virgin.net

Anne Jenkins
2 Windermere Road, Carnforth, Lancs., LA5 9AR
Tel. 01524 734797 Email: anne@jenkins.abelgratis.com

UK Website: www.gearedforgrowth.co.uk

MOSES . . . . . .

55

Christian Focus Publications

publishes books for all ages

Our mission statement –

STAYING FAITHFUL

In dependence upon God we seek to help make His infallible word, the Bible, relevant. Our aim is to ensure that the Lord Jesus Christ is presented as the only hope to obtain forgiveness of sin, live a useful life and look forward to heaven with Him.

REACHING OUT

Christ's last command requires us to reach out to our world with His gospel. We seek to help fulfil that by publishing books that point people towards Jesus and help them develop a Christ-like maturity. We aim to equip all levels of readers for life, work, ministry and mission.

Books in our adult range are published in three imprints.

Christian Focus contains popular works including biographies, commentaries, basic doctrine, and Christian living. Our children's books are also published in this imprint.

Mentor focuses on books written at a level suitable for Bible College and seminary students, pastors, and other serious readers; the imprint includes commentaries, doctrinal studies, examination of current issues, and church history.

Christian Heritage contains classic writings from the past.

For details of our titles visit us on our website
www.christianfocus.com

Christian Focus Publications, Ltd
Geanies House, Fearn,
Ross-shire, IV20 ITW, Scotland, United Kingdom
info@christianfocus.com